SPECIAL CATECHISMS
FOR SPECIAL KIDS

SPECIAL CATECHISMS FOR SPECIAL KIDS
Teaching autistic children about God

Caroline Weerstra

Catechism for Kids
Visit our website
www.catechismforkids.com

To Kevin

I have no greater joy than to hear that my children are walking in the truth. (III John 1:4)

Kevin, this means that Mom is really happy that you know and love Jesus.

CONTENTS

THE STORY

When my son Kevin was born, I thought he was perfect.

"Ten fingers and ten toes," the doctor proclaimed as he lifted my son so that I could see him for the first time. "He is beautiful."

He *was* beautiful. He was beautiful in an almost eerie way. He was silent and still, staring up at the world with eyes that seemed to be contemplating great mysteries. His face glowed with an unearthly quality. People often commented that he looked like the pictures of the Christ child in Renaissance art—as if the only thing missing was the halo around his head.

It stuck in my mind, however, that something was wrong with this unusually beautiful and peaceful child. I had grown up as the oldest daughter in a family of nine children. I had seen my share of babies, and none of them appeared so uncommunicative and out-of-touch with the world around them. The impression only deepened when I brought my son for his first set of immunizations.

The nurse called in an assistant to hold his little hands and legs while the shots were administered. Everyone braced themselves for screams, but there was only silence. He looked up at the ceiling with his deep brown eyes and never blinked.

"What a good baby!" said the nurse.

I felt queasy.

My son's pediatrician assured me that everything was fine. "He is a good baby, a quiet baby," the doctor said. "You should be thankful."

When my son turned two, I reflected that very little had changed. He had learned to sit and crawl and walk on schedule. Still, he stared at the world through strangely serene eyes. He looked up at the clouds and studied the shadows of his fingers against a wall. But he never uttered more than a word or two of understandable speech. Now he had developed strange gibberish that sounded like a Pentecostal tongues-speaking service. I took him back to the doctor.

"He is fine!" the pediatrician informed me impatiently. "Mothers will worry, but I am telling you, Mrs. Weerstra, you have a perfectly healthy son. Children learn at different rates. Give him time, and just try to relax!"

I put my fears aside for a time and convinced myself that it must indeed be as everyone said—Kevin was fine. Perhaps he was even unusually intelligent. Maybe that was why he stared around him with such contemplation. Perhaps he would one day be a great scientist or a famous composer. Everyone said he was fine.

However, as he got older and still could not talk, I struggled more to believe that.

When my son was almost four years old, he finally received the diagnosis that, by then, I had already guessed: autism. I shrugged bitterly when I heard the news. "I'm glad you finally caught up," I told the doctor scornfully, and I shoved the information papers that he held out back into his hands. "I've read it already. I've read it all. I couldn't wait for you."

I tried to be stoic about it, but at home watching my little son stare vacantly at shadows on the wall, I cried. Would I ever be able to communicate with him?

I have always been unconventional with education. As a child, I was bored in school with the endless repetition of trivia that I mostly already knew. I killed time in class by reading and memorizing. I hid books of poems inside my social studies book and committed them to memory. I read ahead in my literature books and memorized my favorite Bible chapters.

The reading and memorization had a downside, however. Adults often chuckled over my use of enormous words like 'wondrous' and 'dilapidated.' Classmates sometimes teased me that I spoke like an encyclopedia, but I had the last laugh whenever we faced down standardized testing in language arts. The words that befuddled so many of my classmates came quite naturally to me.

I had looked forward to reading to my children and hoped to foster in them also the love of words and the art of language.

Now I pulled my four-year-old son onto the couch next to me and offered him a simple storybook. "Do you want Mommy to read to you? Let's read, Sweetie." I opened the book. "Once upon a time …"

He was not listening. He never seemed to hear me at all. He glanced at the pages and put his hand over my mouth, as if to stop me from speaking. Then he began to flip the pages quickly, entertaining himself with the swish of the paper and the breeze that it stirred up in his hair. Story-time was over.

I was sad that I could not read storybooks to my child, but another dilemma haunted me still more. Without an ability to understand stories, my son could make nothing at all of Sunday School. Every Sunday, I would drop him off with the other children, and every Sunday he would sit for a few minutes in his chair, staring at the wall, and then he would get up and wander aimlessly around the room while the teacher told Bible stories to the other children. By the time he was six, he still knew not a single thing about God.

In time, with much work at school and at home, Kevin began to improve his vocabulary and to construct simple sentences. Still, his language comprehension was limited to short phrases composed of commonly-used words. He could make nothing at all of lengthy narrative, and he lacked the attention span to even try. He would sit earnestly in his chair at the beginning of Sunday School, but then his attention would be seized by the ceiling fan or the curtains swaying gently in the spring air, and he lost the gist of the story.

When he was nine, he was a happy, well-adjusted autistic child. He attended church and was loved and accepted by the congregation, but he still knew nothing about God. I threw myself into feverish attempts to teach him something. Eventually, I had tried everything that conventional education had for a child. Kevin could not understand the Westminster Shorter Catechism. He could not understand most of the Catechism for Young Children. He could not understand Bible stories. He was now twelve, and he was old enough to feel embarrassed about being put in classes with younger children and being given books with preschool-level cartoon pictures. It all made little difference anyway, because he understood none of it.

In frustration, I sat down again to talk the matter over with my husband. "There is nothing for him," I said. "I tried to start him on a first-grade Bible story book. He said it was for babies because of all the cartoon pictures. I don't blame him, but I don't know what to do. I made him sit still and listen for a few pages, but he didn't understand it anyway."

"Well," my husband said, "maybe we should think of this another way. We know what doesn't work. What *would* work? What could he understand? Is there something that we could put together for him that would help him learn?"

I began to think of the sort of thing that Kevin *could* understand. He needed short sentences—something in normal everyday English with no big words. He needed a book that looked like it was for older children, so that he would not be embarrassed to carry it around. He needed repetition, so that he heard something not once or twice, but every day until he could remember it. He needed a special catechism.

When I first began teaching my son the catechism, I wondered whether he would understand even this simplified version. Would he be able to remember it from one day to the next? And even more importantly, would he understand it or would he be merely repeating a meaningless jumble of words?

The first two questions were quickly answered. Kevin seemed quite pleased at being more included in daily devotions. He loved learning to correctly answer his questions. Although his learning pace was slower than that of a normal child, he eventually mastered question after question. "God made everything ... God made me ... God made me for his glory," he would lisp in his sweet but stammering voice. Still, I wondered whether he knew what he was saying.

One day, I visited his class for the annual parent-teacher meeting. Kevin's teacher gave me all the usual information about his schoolwork and grades, and then she smiled at me oddly and asked, "And how are things for him at church?"

"At church?" I asked, surprised. "Fine, I guess."

"He has become very interested in God lately," she added, smiling more broadly now. "I have the most religious class in the school because of your son. He is always going around to the other children and telling them about Jesus."

"He is?" I was stunned.

"Oh, yes. He tells them that God made everyone and everything, and that they should believe in God. It's okay. I really don't mind. It is sweet. He obviously really enjoys church."

"He doesn't disrupt the class with it, does

he?" I worried.

"Oh no," she said. "In fact, it is helpful sometimes. Whenever someone does something mean to another kid, Kevin goes over and says, 'I will pray for you.'"

"To the kid who is crying?"

"No, actually, he says it to the child who is misbehaving. And then he does it, too. Right then and there. He says, 'Jesus, please help my friend understand that what he did was wrong. Please change his heart and help him to obey your rules. Amen.' Kids aren't as mean to each other anymore because they know that Kevin will come over to pray for them."

My son was fourteen when he made his profession of faith. In two years, he had gone from barely even knowing the existence of God to being able to explain to others that Jesus had died for his sins. At the examination, Kevin sat in front of the elders with his still-beautiful eyes glowing and lisped the answers to every question that they put to him.

"When we take the Lord's Supper, what does the bread represent?"

"Jesus' body that was broken for us."

"And what does the wine represent?"

Kevin paused, and then a sly grin broke out across his face. "Pastor Tom, we do not use wine in our church. We use grape juice."

The elders laughed uproariously. "Yes, that's right! We do! And what does the juice represent?"

"It represents Jesus' blood that was poured out for us."

"And why did Jesus die on the cross for your sins?"

"Because he loves me."

THE METHOD

The catechism method is not an innovation. In fact, this method has been used to great effect with all sorts of children for centuries. In many churches even today, children are taught to repeat the words of the Westminster Shorter Catechism or the Heidelberg Catechism as part of their Christian education. Children often learn to recite the catechism before they fully understand the meaning of the words. The comprehension develops in time as the same phrases are repeated again and again.

Special Catechisms for Special Kids employs the same concept with a slight modification. Autistic children are and probably will always be seriously impaired in language comprehension. Other children may eventually learn the meaning of this sentence:

> *God is a Spirit, infinite, eternal, and unchangeable, in his being, wisdom, power, holiness, justice, goodness, and truth.*

An autistic child, on the other hand, is unlikely to

ever fully comprehend it. It is simply too long, too complex, and the words are unfamiliar. The same concept of God, however, can be presented in a series of shorter sentences:

> *"Where is God?"*
> *"Everywhere."*
>
> *"Can you see God?"*
> *"No, but God can see me."*
>
> *"Can God see everything?"*
> *"Yes."*
>
> *"Does God know everything?"*
> *"Yes."*
>
> *"Can God do anything?"*
> *"Yes."*
>
> *"How long does God live?"*
> *"Forever and ever."*

The most important point is not whether an autistic child can say 'infinite, eternal, and unchangeable,' but rather whether the child understands in substance that God is infinite, eternal, and unchangeable, although the child might use simpler words to describe it.

How should I begin?

Choose a catechism from this book for your

child. Most people begin with the first one, because it is the simplest and most basic.

Once you have chosen a catechism, sit down with your child in the setting that is most relaxing for him or her. Some children do well sitting at a desk, while some can concentrate better when they are allowed to stand up or even play with a favorite toy. Ask your child the catechism questions and then assist in providing the answer. Repetition is the key to catechism learning. Repeat, repeat, repeat. Repeat every day, if possible, or at least three times a week. You can pass time in the car or waiting for an appointment by asking your child the catechism questions. Although it seems unlikely at first, most mild or moderately autistic children *can* learn these. Eventually, the child will not need your assistance to remember the answers to the questions.

Once your child becomes accustomed to learning catechism, the process generally moves more quickly, and you may not need to repeat as much or as often.

Do I begin with one catechism question or a whole set?

This depends on your child and his or her particular level. Some autistic children become confused when presented with more than one question at a time, while other children become bored being asked to repeat only one question over and over. Try your child on one or two questions to begin, and work up from there.

Why are some questions repeated in several catechisms?

Autistic children tend to be rigid thinkers. When teaching an autistic child a particular principle, it is important to be sure that the child recognizes that it may be applied to multiple situations or considered from several different angles. The use of the same questions in different catechisms assists the autistic child in comprehending and applying the concepts.

Should I reward my child for learning the catechism?

It is often helpful to offer small rewards as motivation. Autistic children may be quite unmoved by the usual parental praise ("Good job!"), but they may respond well to stickers or small toys or outings to the park. It is NOT recommended that any parent punish a child for failing to learn the catechism. Autistic children are often severely handicapped in their ability to learn language, and it may be difficult for them to recall the answers, especially when they first begin the program. Punishment may only discourage the child and give him or her a negative attitude toward religious training. Patience is needed to teach any child, and especially an autistic child. In the end, however, the rewards are well worth the difficulties.

What should I do if my child cannot understand even the modified catechism?

The catechisms in this book are written for mild to moderately autistic children. Some children who suffer from more severe forms of autism may not be able to understand them. Since even mild to moderately autistic children vary in their comprehension level, some children may need further modification of the catechisms. If substituting a few words or adding in a few extra questions and answers improves your child's comprehension of the concepts, feel free to make these alterations to your program.

How long does it take?

The catechism method takes only a few minutes per day. However, it is important to keep up with it every day in order to see significant progress.

THE CATECHISMS

CATECHISM ONE
WHO MADE YOU?

Q1. Who made everything?
  A. God made everything.

Q2. Did God make the stars?
  A. Yes.

Q3. Did God make the sun?
  A. Yes.

Q4. Did God make the moon?
  A. Yes.

Q5. Did God make the ocean?
  A. Yes.

Q6. Did God make the fish that swim in
     the ocean?
  A. Yes.

Q7. Did God make the trees and flowers?
  A. Yes.

Q8. Did God make the animals?
  A. Yes.

Q9. Who made you?
  A. God made me.

Q10. Why did God make you?
  A. God made me for his glory.

CATECHISM TWO
WHO IS GOD? (Part 1)

Q1. Who made you?
   A. God made me.

Q2. Where is God?
   A. God is everywhere.

Q3. Can you see God?
   A. No, but God can see me.

Q4. How many Gods are there?
   A. There is one God.

Q5. How many persons are there in God?
   A. Three.

Q6. Who are those three?
   A. The Father, the Son, and the Holy Spirit.

Q7. Is the Father God?
  A. Yes.

Q8. Is the Son God?
  A. Yes.

Q9. Is the Holy Spirit God?
  A. Yes.

Q10. Which one is Jesus?
  A. Jesus is the Son.

Repeat Q4 for emphasis:
    How many Gods are there?
        A. There is one God.

CATECHISM THREE
WHO IS GOD? (Part 2)

Q1. Where is God?
  A. Everywhere.

Q2. Can you see God?
  A. No, but God can see me.

Q3. Can God see everything?
  A. Yes.

Q4. Does God know everything?
  A. Yes.

Q5. Can God do anything?
  A. Yes.

Q6. How long does God live?
  A. Forever and ever.

Q7. Is God good?
  A. Yes, God is good.

Q8. Is God always good?

   A. Yes, God is always good.

Q9. Will God ever change and become bad?

   A. No, God will never change.

Q10. Can you trust God?

   A. Yes, I can always trust God.

CATECHISM FOUR
NAMES OF JESUS

Q1. Why do we call Jesus our 'Lord'?
  A. Because he is our king.

Q2. Why do we call Jesus our 'Savior'?
  A. Because he saves us from our sins.

Q3. Why do we call Jesus 'Immanuel'?
  A. Because he is God with us.

Q4. Why do we call Jesus 'Christ'?
  A. Because he is the One sent to save us.

Q5. When we talk about our 'Lord', who
      are we talking about?
  A. Jesus.

Q6. When we talk about our 'Savior', who
      are we talking about?
  A. Jesus.

Q7. When we talk about 'Immanuel', who are we talking about?
   A. Jesus.

Q8. When we talk about 'Christ', who are we talking about?
   A. Jesus.

Q9. What does God say about his name?
   A. 'You shall not take the name of the Lord your God in vain.'

Q10. What does 'you shall not take the name of the Lord your God in vain' mean?
   A. It means that I should remember that God's name is special. When I say his name, I should remember that I am talking about God.

CATECHISM FIVE
THE BIRTH OF JESUS

Q1. Who told Mary that she would have a
  baby?
  A. An angel told her.

Q2. What did the angel tell her about the
  baby?
  A. The angel said that the baby was the Son
  of God.

Q3. Mary was about to get married. Who
  was she going to marry?
  A. Joseph.

Q4. Was Joseph the father of Jesus?
  A. No, God is the Father of Jesus.

Q5. Where was Jesus born?
  A. In a stable in Bethlehem.

Q6. What is a stable?
  A. A stable is a barn.

Q7. Where did Mary put baby Jesus?
  A. In a manger.

Q8. What is a manger?
  A. A manger is a place to put hay for the animals to eat.

Q9. Why did Mary put Jesus in a manger?
  A. Because there are no beds in a barn.

Q10. Why did God send his Son Jesus to be born as a baby in Bethlehem?
  A. To save us from our sins.

Q11. Who first heard the good news that Jesus was born?
  A. Shepherds in the field.

Q12. What are shepherds?
  A. Shepherds take care of sheep.

Q13. Who told the shepherds that Jesus was born?
  A. Angels.

Q14. What did the angels say?
   A. Glory to God in the highest and on earth peace, goodwill toward men.

Q15. What did the shepherds do when they heard the news?
   A. They went to Bethlehem to see Jesus, and they told everyone about Jesus.

Q16. Who else went to see Jesus?
   A. The Wise Men.

Q17. Who were the Wise Men?
   A. Kings from the east.

Q18. How did the Wise Men know where to find Jesus?
   A. They followed a star.

Q19. What did they do when they saw Jesus?
   A. They worshiped him and gave him gifts.

Q20. What gifts did they bring him?
   A. Gold, frankincense, and myrrh.

CATECHISM SIX
THE DEATH AND RESURRECTION OF JESUS

Q1. Where did Jesus die?
  A. At Calvary.

Q2. How did Jesus die?
  A. He was crucified.

Q3. What does 'crucified' mean?
  A. It means that his hands and feet were nailed to a cross.

Q4. Had Jesus done anything wrong?
  A. No, never.

Q5. What did Jesus say about the people who crucified Him?
  A. "Father, forgive them, for they do not know what they are doing."

Q6. What were they doing?
  A. They were killing the Son of God.

Q7. What did Jesus say before he died?
  A. "Into your hands I commend my
     spirit."

Q8. Was Jesus helpless to save himself?
  A. No, he could have called an army of
     angels to fight for him.

Q9. Jesus did not call angels to fight for
     him. Why did he let evil men kill him?
  A. To pay for our sins.

Q10. Did Jesus pay for your sins at Calvary?
  A. Yes, Jesus paid for my sins.

Q11. How was Jesus buried?
  A. He was wrapped in cloth and placed
     in a tomb.

Q12. What was placed in the doorway of
     the tomb?
  A. A stone.

Q13. How many days was Jesus in the tomb?
  A. Three days.

Q14. What happened on the third day?
  A. He rose from the dead.

Q15. How do we know that Jesus rose
      from the dead?
  A. His friends saw him alive. He spoke
      to them and ate with them.

Q16. What happened forty days after
      Jesus rose from the dead?
  A. He went up into heaven.

Q17. Where is Jesus now?
  A. In heaven at the right hand of God
      the Father.

Q18. What is Jesus doing now?
  A. He is making intercession for us.

Q19. What does it mean to say that Jesus
      makes intercession for us?
  A. He prays for us.

Q20. Why did Jesus die and rise again?
  A. Because he loves us.

CATECHISM SEVEN
SALVATION

Q1. What is sin?
  A. Sin is breaking God's rules.

Q2. Do you sin?
  A. Yes, everybody sins.

Q3. What should you do when you sin?
  A. Pray and ask God to forgive me.

Q4. What else should you do when you sin?
  A. If I hurt someone or made them sad,
     I should say I am sorry and that I will
     not do that again, God helping me.

Q5. Does God forgive you?
  A. Yes.

Q6. Why does God forgive you?
  A. Because Jesus paid for my sins on the
     cross.

Q7. Why did Jesus die on the cross for your sins?
A. Because he loves me.

Q8. Do other people sin?
A. Yes, everyone sins.

Q9. If someone sins and says they are sorry, what should you do?
A. I should forgive them.

Q10. If someone sins and does not say they are sorry, what should you do?
A. I should pray that God will change their heart so that they will be sorry for their sin.

CATECHISM EIGHT
TEN COMMANDMENTS

Q1. What are the Ten Commandments?
  A. God's rules.

Q2. Does God want you to obey the Ten Commandments?
  A. Yes, God wants everyone to obey the Ten Commandments.

Q3. What is the first commandment?
  A. 'You shall have no other gods before Me.'

Q4. What does 'you shall have no other gods before Me' mean?
  A. It means that I should pray only to God, and I should love God more than anything else.

Q5. What is the second commandment?
  A. 'You shall make no graven images.'

Q6. What does 'you shall make no graven images' mean?
  A. It means that I should only worship God the way that the Bible tells me to worship him.

Q7. What is the third commandment?
  A. 'You shall not take the name of the Lord your God in vain.'

Q8. What does 'you shall not take the name of the Lord your God in vain' mean?
  A. It means that I should remember that God's name is special. When I say his name, I should remember that I am talking about God.

Q9. What is the fourth commandment?
  A. 'Remember the Sabbath Day to keep it holy.'

Q10. What does 'remember the Sabbath Day to keep it holy' mean?
  A. It means that I should rest and honor God on Sunday because it is the Lord's Day.

Q11. What is the fifth commandment?
  A. 'Honor your mother and father.'

Q12. What does 'honor your mother and father' mean?
  A. It means that I should obey my mother and father when I am young and take care of them when they are old.

Q13. What is the sixth commandment?
  A. 'You shall not kill.'

Q14. What does 'you shall not kill' mean?
  A. It means that I should never hurt or kill anyone, and I should always be kind to people.

Q15. What is the seventh commandment?
  A. 'You shall not commit adultery.'

Q16. What does 'you shall not commit adultery' mean?
  A. It means that God wants husbands and wives to stay together and not have other boyfriends or girlfriends after they are married.

Q17. What is the eighth commandment?
  A. 'You shall not steal.'

Q18. What does 'you shall not steal' mean?
A. It means that I should not take something that does not belong to me without asking.

Q19. What is the ninth commandment?
A. 'You shall not bear false witness.'

Q20. What does 'you shall not bear false witness' mean?
A. It means that I should never tell a lie about someone to hurt them.

Q21. What is the tenth commandment?
A. 'You shall not covet.'

Q22. What does 'you shall not covet' mean?
A. It means that I should not be angry when other people have nice things. I should be happy for them.

Q23. What is sin?
A. Sin is breaking God's rules.

Q24. Do you sin?
A. Yes, everyone sins.

Q25. What should you do when you sin?
A. Pray and ask God to forgive me.

Q26. Does God forgive you?
   A. Yes.

Q27. Why does God forgive you?
   A. Because Jesus paid for my sins on
      the cross.

Q28. Why did Jesus die on the cross for
      your sins?
   A. Because he loves me.

Q29. Can you ever pay for your own sins?
   A. No, never. Only Jesus can pay for
      my sins.

Q30. What should you do because Jesus
      loves you and forgave your sins?
   A. I should love God and obey his
      rules.

CATECHISM NINE
BAPTISM

Q1. What is baptism?
 A. Baptism is when water is sprinkled on my head to show that I belong to God.

Q2. What does the water mean?
 A. It means that Jesus has washed my sins away.

Q3. How did Jesus wash your sins away?
 A. He paid for my sins on the cross.

Q4. What words does your pastor say when he baptizes you?
 A. 'I baptize you in the name of the Father, and of the Son, and of the Holy Spirit.'

Q5. Why does he say that?
 A. To show that my baptism is given to me by God—the Father, the Son, and the Holy Spirit.

Q6. How many times do you get baptized?
 A. Only one time.

Q7. Why only one time?
 A. Because I belong to God forever, and
     he does not let me go.

Q8. Is baptism scary?
 A. No, it is only a little bit of water, and
     my mom and dad will be there with
     me. It does not hurt at all.

Q9. Is it a good thing to be baptized?
 A. It is a very good thing, and everyone
     will be very happy for me.

Q10. What should you do after you are
      baptized?
  A. I should always remember that I belong
      to God.

CATECHISM TEN
PROFESSION OF FAITH

Q1. What is profession of faith?
  A. Profession of faith is when I tell the
     church that I promise to love and
     obey God all my life.

Q2. What do you need to do before you
     give your profession of faith?
  A. I need to learn about God.

Q3. And then what will you do?
  A. I have an interview with the elders at
     my church.

Q4. What happens at your interview?
  A. I talk to the elders of the church and
     tell them all the things I have learned
     about God.

Q5. What else do you tell them?
  A. I tell them that I love God and believe in God.

Q6. What will the elders do if you do not pass your interview?
  A. They will give me time to learn more about God.

Q7. What will the elders do if you pass your interview?
  A. They will let me make my profession of faith.

Q8. Do you need to be scared about your interview?
  A. No.

Q9. Why not?
  A. The elders are nice, and they are helping me.

Q10. What happens on the day of your profession of faith?
  A. I will stand in the front of the church and make my promises.

Q11. What will you promise?
  A. I will promise that I believe in God
      and in the Bible, and I will promise
      to love and obey God all my life.

See Appendix for specific Profession of Faith vows.

CATECHISM ELEVEN
LORD'S SUPPER

Q1. What is the Lord's Supper?
  A. The Lord's supper is when we eat the bread and drink the wine at church.

Q2. Who told us to take the Lord's Supper?
  A. Jesus.

Q3. Why did Jesus tell us to take the Lord's Supper?
  A. To remember him.

Q4. What does the bread represent?
  A. Jesus' body that was broken for us.

Q5. What does the wine represent?
  A. Jesus' blood that was poured out for us.

Q6. When was Jesus' body broken for you?
  A. When he died on the cross for my sins.

Q7. When was Jesus' blood poured out for you?
  A. When he died on the cross for my sins.

Q8. Why did Jesus die on the cross for your sins?
  A. Because he loves me.

Q9. What should you do before you eat the bread and drink the wine?
  A. I should ask God to forgive me for my sins, and I should thank God for his love.

CATECHISM TWELVE
LORD'S PRAYER

Q1. What is prayer?
  A. Prayer is talking to God.

Q2. Can you pray?
  A. Yes.

Q3. Where can you pray?
  A. Anywhere. God can always hear me.

Q4. Do you have to talk out loud for God to hear you?
  A. No, God knows what I am thinking.

Q5. What can you pray about?
  A. I can thank God for good things, and I can ask him for things that I need.

Q6. Can you pray for other people?
  A. Yes, I can ask God to help other people.

Q7. What is the Lord's Prayer?
  A. The Lord's Prayer is a prayer that
     Jesus told us to pray.

Q8. How does the Lord's Prayer begin?
  A. 'Our Father who art in heaven'

Q9. What does 'our Father who art in
     heaven' mean?
  A. It means that I can talk to God like he
     is my father.

Q10. What is the next part of the Lord's
      prayer?
   A. 'Hallowed be thy name.'

Q11. What does 'hallowed be thy name'
      mean?
   A. It means that I should always
      remember that God's name is
      special.

Q12. What is the next part of the Lord's
      prayer?
   A. 'Thy kingdom come.'

Q13. What does 'thy kingdom come' mean?
A. It means that I pray that Jesus would be honored as king everywhere.

Q14. What is the next part of the Lord's prayer?
A. 'Thy will be done on earth as it is in heaven.'

Q15. What does 'thy will be done on earth as it is in heaven' mean?
A. It means that I pray that God will help everyone to obey him.

Q16. What is the next part of the Lord's prayer?
A. 'Give us this day our daily bread.'

Q17. What does 'give us this day our daily bread' mean?
A. It means that I pray for the things that I need.

Q18. What is the next part of the Lord's prayer?
A. 'Forgive us our debts as we forgive our debtors.'

Q19. What does 'forgive us our debts as we forgive our debtors mean?'

A. It means that I pray that God will forgive me for my sins and that God will help me to forgive other people for their sins.

Q20. What is the next part of the Lord's prayer?

A. 'And lead us not into temptation, but deliver us from evil.'

Q21. What does 'and lead us not into temptation, but deliver us from evil' mean?

A. It means that I pray that God would help me to not sin.

Q22. What is the last part of the Lord's prayer?

A. 'For thine is the kingdom, and the power, and the glory, forever. Amen.'

Q23. What does 'for thine is the kingdom, and the power, and the glory, forever. Amen' mean?

A. It means that I remember that only God can answer prayers.

Q24. Should you only pray the Lord's prayer?

A. No, I can pray many things, but I should also pray the Lord's prayer.

Q25. Does God hear your prayers?

A. Yes, God always hears my prayers.

APPENDIX

PROFESSION OF FAITH VOWS

In the course of a public profession of faith, the candidate is asked questions that constitute membership vows. These questions can be modified so that they can be better understood by an autistic or other mentally challenged person. Below are suggested modifications of membership vows for several well-known Reformed denominations.

Orthodox Presbyterian Church

Adapted from the OPC Directory for the Public Worship of God.

1. Do you believe that God gave us the Bible? Will you obey the Bible?
2. Are you a sinner? Do you trust Jesus to save you from your sins?
3. Do you promise to love and obey God?
4. Do you promise to listen to your pastor and elders and obey them as they teach you the Word of God?

Presbyterian Church of America

Adapted from the PCA Form of Government.

1. Do you know that you are a sinner?
2. Do you trust Jesus to save you from your sins?
3. Do you promise to love and obey God?
4. Do you promise to love the church and help as much as you can?
5. Do you promise to listen to your pastor and elders and obey them as they teach you the Word of God?

Associate Reformed Presbyterian Church

Adapted from the ARP Form of Government.

1. Do you know that you are a sinner?
2. Do you trust Jesus to save you from your sins?
3. Do you believe that God gave us the Bible? Will you obey the Bible?
4. Do you promise to love and obey God?
5. Do you believe that the Associate Reformed Presbyterian Church teaches the truth about God?
6. Do you promise to obey God at home and at church?
7. Do you promise to listen to your pastor and elders and obey them as they teach you the Word of God?

Made in the USA
Lexington, KY
20 April 2011